✂ MATH ALIVE ✂

# BUILDING
# MATH

## JOHN PERRITANO

**Marshall Cavendish**
Benchmark
New York

10-08

Marshall Cavendish Benchmark
99 White Plains Road
Tarrytown, NY 10591
www.marshallcavendish.us

**Library of Congress Cataloging-in-Publication Data**
Perritano, John.
Building math / by John Perritano.
p. cm. -- (Math alive)
Includes bibliographical references and index.
ISBN 978-0-7614-3210-4
1.  Engineering mathematics--Juvenile literature. 2.  Engineering
mathematics--Experiments--Juvenile literature. I. Title.
TA330.P47 2009
510--dc22
2008014559

The photographs in this book are used by permission and through
the courtesy of:

Bryan Busovicki/ Shutterstock: 4-5, Pichugin Dmitry/ Shutterstock: 6-7, Andr
Klaassen/Shutterstock: 8-9, Wong Tsu Shi/ Shutterstock: 10-11, Styve Reineck/
Shutterstock: 12, Donald R. Swartz/ Shutterstock: 14, Associated Press: 15,
Mike Liu/ Shutterstock: 16-17, Joshua Haviv/ Shutterstock: 18-19,  Museum of
the City of New York/ Getty Images: 19t, Kevin Connors: 20, Associated Press:
22-23, Allen Furmanski/ Shutterstock: 24, Qaphotos/ Alamy: 26-27, Michael
Thompson/ Dreamstime: 28.
Illustrations: Q2AMedia Art Bank
Cover Photo: Front: Yakobchuk Vasyl/ Shutterstock.
Back: UltraOrto, S.A./ Shutterstock.
Half Title: Styve Reineck/ Shutterstock.
Creative Director: Simmi Sikka
Series Editor: Jessica Cohn
Art Director: Sudakshina Basu
Designers: Dibakar Acharjee and Prashant Kumar
Illustrators: Indranil Ganguly, Rishi Bhardwaj, Kusum Kala and  Pooja Shukla
Photo research: Sejal Sehgal
Senior Project Manager: Ravneet Kaur
Project Manager: Shekhar Kapur

Printed in Malaysia
1 3 5 6 4 2

# Contents

# Ancient Structures

Buildings are not just made of materials like bricks and steel. Plenty of math goes into making them, too. This is true for the newest skyscrapers. It is also true for ancient buildings in Greece, Egypt, and elsewhere. Without mathematical thinking and **equations**, nothing would ever be built.

## The Wonder of Rome

The Romans constructed magnificent buildings. The Roman Coliseum was the greatest stadium of the ancient world. It was built between the years 70 C.E. and 80 C.E. The Romans held sporting events in the 50,000-seat Coliseum. The stadium played host to huge public events, such as mock sea battles.

### Coliseum Dimensions

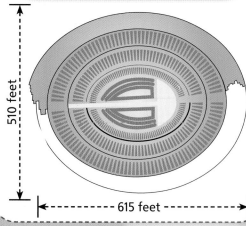

510 feet

615 feet

*Diagram is not to scale

How did the industrious Romans build these giant structures? It wasn't easy. These civilizations didn't have the benefit of advanced materials, methods, and machines. The Romans built their civilizations using the tools of their time. Ancient engineers got the job done using simple tools and many of the same math principles builders use today.

## Calculation Station

Measurements in the ancient world were often based on their relationship with human body parts. The basic unit was the **cubit**. The cubit was calculated by measuring the distance between a man's elbow and his fingertips. By today's U.S. measure, that would be about 18 inches. The average height of an adult man was measured as four cubits in ancient times.

Another ancient measure was the palm. That was based on the size of a man's palm. What would the size of a palm be in inches? A yard is equal to three feet, or 36 inches. If a yard equals 12 palms, how many inches are in a palm? (Answer is on page 31.)

▼ The arena inside was an ellipse, which is like a flattened circle.

# Egyptian Pyramids

Perhaps no ancient building is more famous than the Great Pyramid at Giza, Egypt. The Great Pyramid was built for King Khufu about 4,500 years ago. Pyramids are four-sided structures with a square base.

The Great Pyramid was built with more than 2 million limestone blocks. The blocks range in weight from 2.5 tons to 15 tons. Two hundred layers of block make up the entire structure. The Egyptians carved the stones so that they would fit tightly. Not even a credit card can fit between the blocks. Construction on this marvel took about twenty years.

# How Was It Built?

Since records do not tell how the Egyptians built the pyramid, scientists have different thoughts about how it was done. Some say the Egyptians used ramps to put the stones in place. Ramps are surfaces that slope. They make it easier to move weighty objects to a specific height.

At the start, the Great Pyramid stood 481 feet (147 meters) high. Its base covers almost fourteen acres. That is equal to several New York City blocks. The pyramid's four corners are built to point like a compass. The corners point to the north, south, east, and west.

## Calculation Station

The Great Pyramid has a square base that measures about 252 yards on each side. To calculate the **area** of a square, multiply the length of one side by itself. What would the area be, in yards, for the base of the Great Pyramid? (Answer is on page 31.)

## Great Pyramid Dimensions

148 meters

230 meters

*Diagram is not to scale

◀ The Great Pyramid has worn down nearly 35 feet (11 meters) over time.

# Birth of Geometry

The Great Pyramid walls are made of four **equilateral** triangles. The base is a square. At the time of construction, the Egyptians had already developed the branch of mathematics called **geometry**. Geometry is the study of space, or the study of **two-dimensional** and **three-dimensional** figures.

Oddly enough, the Egyptians did not know how large their pyramid was. A Greek mathematician named Thales finally figured it out. Thales waited for the time of day when the length of his shadow equaled his own height. When that time of the day came, he measured the pyramid's shadow. He knew that the length of the Great Pyramid's shadow would also equal its height.

▲ Scientists are still trying to figure out where the 20,000 to 30,000 pyramid workers lived.

# Hands-On Math: Build a Pyramid

Follow these directions and build a pyramid of your own.

## What You Will Need:

- 8-1/2-inch × 11-inch sheet of paper
- Scissors
- Blue pencil
- Ruler
- Red pencil
- Tape

## What to Do:

**1** Fold one corner of the paper to the opposite side. Cut off the extra so you have an 8-1/2-inch square.

**2** Fold the square in half. Fold it in half again. Then open it.

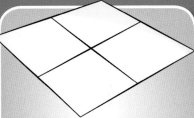

**3** Mark the middle points on each side. Draw two lines connecting the opposite center points.

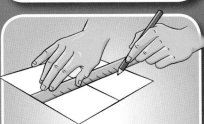

**4** From the center, measure 3-1/4 inches outward along each of the four shorter lines.

**5** Draw a red line from each corner of the square to the points just marked to the right and left of each corner.

**6** Cut along the red lines. Throw the scrap paper away.

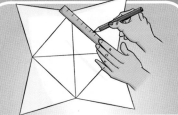

**7** Draw blue lines, as shown in the diagram.

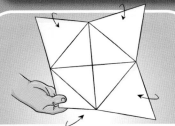

**8** Fold along the blue lines. Tape the edges together.

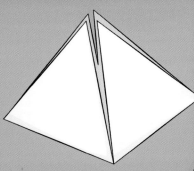

# The Great Wall of China

The Great Wall of China was built about 2,500 years ago. Some of its sections are in ruins. Yet the parts that still stand are amazing. The Great Wall can even be seen from space at times.

The 4,163-mile (6,700-kilometer) wall was built when China was a series of separate states. The Chinese connected several walls in the northern part of the country to defend against attacks.

## Rocks and Earth

Constructed mostly of rocks, stones, and packed earth, the Great Wall stretches from Bo Hai Bay, on the eastern coast, to Gansu province. That is in the western desert. The wall's width, or thickness, ranges from about 16 feet to 30 feet (5 meters to 9 meters). The wall is 39 feet (12 meters) at its highest point.

**Location**

Beijing

CHINA

The Chinese built much of the wall by pounding earth between board frames. They used roughly 393 million cubic yards (300 million cubic meters) of soil during construction.

The Chinese also used bricks. Bricks could bear the weight of the wall better than many other materials. Bricks are strong because their material is smashed together. Each brick can stand up to a lot of weight. Stone was often the material of choice, too. They used stones cut into rectangular shapes to form the base.

◀ Armies of peasants, soldiers, and prisoners built the Great Wall.

## Calculation Station

The Greek mathematician Pythagoras lived about 2,500 years ago. He is known as the "Father of Numbers." One of his most famous equations has to do with right triangles, which are triangles that have one **right angle**.

Identify the right angle in this triangle. (Answer is on page 31.)

The sum of the squares of the lengths of legs "a" and "b" in the right triangle (as shown above) is equal to the square of the length of leg "c" or $a^2 + b^2 = c^2$.

# The Parthenon

The Parthenon is yet another famous ancient building. The ancient Greeks built the Parthenon in Athens. Construction began in 447 B.C.E. That means it was started 447 years before the year 1 C.E.! To figure out how many years ago that was, add the number of the current year to 447.

# Optical Illusion

The architects wanted the building to look perfect. So, they built the temple with forty-six outside columns and without any right angles or straight lines. Each of the outside columns has a slight bend. All lean inward.

They built the temple that way to correct a common optical illusion. When seen against the sky, a straight column looks as if it grows narrow in the middle.

The Parthenon is a classic show of **symmetry**. In other words, if you cut the Parthenon in half, one side would look the same as the other side.

◄ The marble used in the Parthenon weighed 22,000 tons.

# Hands-On Math: Paper Towel Columns

Columns can hold heavy loads, such as the roof of the Parthenon. Some kinds of columns are better and stronger than others. Let's see if a paper tube can withstand the load caused by your weight.

## What You Will Need:

- Cookie sheet or oven tray
- Masking tape
- Empty paper towel tube
- Sturdy chair
- Sand or salt
- Funnel

## What to Do:

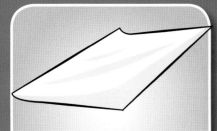

**1** Place the cookie sheet or tray on the floor.

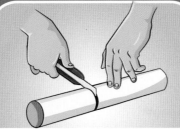

**2** Get an adult to cut the paper towel tube in half, so you have two tubes.

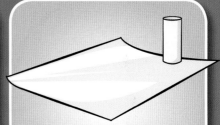

**3** Place one empty tube on the tray so it stands on one end.

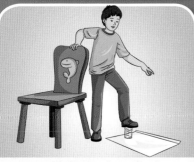

**4** Holding the chair back, slowly press down on the top of the tube with one foot.

**5** Press until the column collapses. Rate its strength as weak, fair, good, or strong.

**6** Try taping the second tube on the tray. Pour salt or sand inside, using a funnel. Repeat steps 2 through 5.

## Explain Away

*The second tube was rated as stronger than the first one. Why ? (Answer is on page 31.)*

# Skyscrapers and Bridges

Walter Chrysler and John J. Raskob started a race in 1929. Each wanted to build the world's tallest building. Raskob's 102-story Empire State Building beat the Chrysler Building in height by 204 feet (62 meters). Both structures were built in New York City.

◀ It took one year and 45 days to build the Empire State Building.

## Inside Look

The Empire State Building rose an average of four and a half stories each week. Workers needed 730 tons of aluminum and stainless steel. Limestone and granite went into the walls, along with the metal. Each material added to the skyscraper's **stability**. Steel, for example, can

### Height of Empire State Building

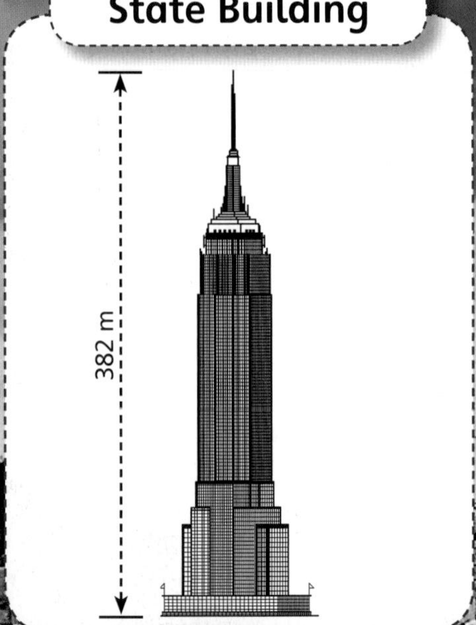

382 m

*Diagram is not to scale

withstand the forces that cause **tension** and **compression**. Tension is the stretching force that pulls on an object. Too much tension and *snap!* the object breaks. Compression is the force that squeezes materials together.

Inside the building, steel columns and beams form a stable **grid**. A grid that is drawn on paper shows many lines going up and down and many others going across. A grid in a building works the same way. Workers closely spaced each column. The lower columns are pushed downward by the weight above. Those columns have to be able to withstand a heavy load.

Builders put many columns and beams in the center. That made a backbone to help the Empire State Building stand against wind forces. A 110-mile-an-hour wind would only make the Empire State Building sway 1.48 inches (3.76 centimeters).

## Calculation Station

There were 3,000 men working on the Empire State Building at one time. Of that number, 255 were carpenters. How many were not carpenters? (Answer is on page 31.)

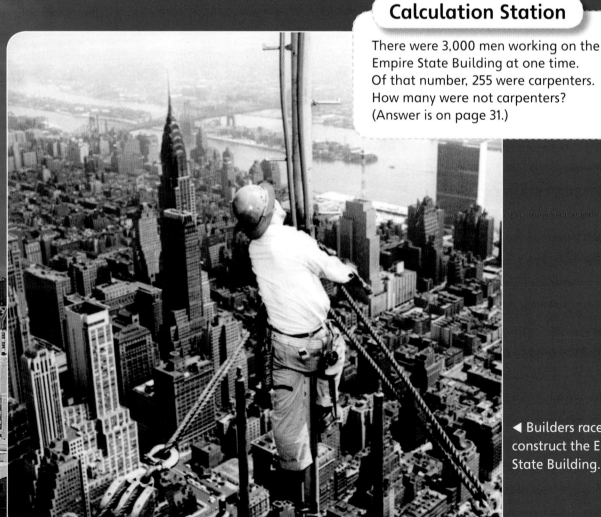

◀ Builders raced to construct the Empire State Building.

# Sears Tower

The Sears Tower opened in Chicago in 1973. At 1,454 feet (443 meters) high, it is a four-sided tower with opposite sides that are equal. Nine square tubes of steel help hold the building together. The sides of these squares are 75 feet (23 meters) high and wide.

The Empire State Building gets its stability from columns and beams in the building's center. The Sears Tower has many columns and beams at the outer walls. This design is just as strong, but weighs much less.

# Wind Stress

Wind causes an enormous amount of **stress** on a skyscraper, especially on the upper floors. The square tubes help all 108 stories withstand the force of blowing wind. That is important because Chicago is called the "Windy City." Wind there blows an average of 16 miles (25 kilometers) per hour. The tubes allow the building to sway just a bit. That helps it soak in some of stress from the wind.

▶The Sears Tower weighs 440 million pounds (200 million kilograms).

# Hands-On Math: A Stable Tower

See if you can make a stable tower out of clay.

## What You Will Need:
• 4 to 6 ounces of clay    • 4 to 5 toothpicks    • Pencil    • Paper

## What to Do:

**1** Mold a tower, in the shape of a **cylinder**, out of clay. Make sure it is the same thickness all the way to the top.

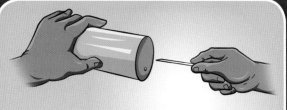

**2** Push two toothpicks into the base until they are flat with the bottom. Stand the tower up and see if they help make it more stable.

**3** Decide where you should place a third toothpick to increase the tower's stability. If the tower is still unstable, use more toothpicks. Write down your observations.

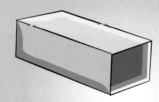

**4** Repeat the experiment with a rectangular tower shape. Make sure it is the same thickness all the way to the top.

## Explain Away
*What can you conclude from this experiment? Write your conclusions down. (Answer is on page 31.)*

# The Brooklyn Bridge

At 5,989 feet (1,825 meters) long, the Brooklyn Bridge was the longest bridge of the nineteenth century. It connects the New York City **boroughs** of Brooklyn and Manhattan. The structure was the idea of engineer John Roebling. He died in 1869, leaving his son, Washington Roebling, to finish the project.

The son's first task was to build the bridge's two massive stone towers. Each of the towers needed to rise hundreds of feet, nearly 85 meters, above the water. To do this, he had to anchor the towers to the bedrock under the riverbed. Bedrock is the solid rock beneath the dirt.

## Compression and Tension

Roebling then strung huge wire cables to keep the bridge from falling down. In **suspension bridges**, the roadway hangs from large cables. He designed his cables to run over the top of the two large towers. He connected them at each end of the bridge.

◄ The roadway hangs from these cables.

**Brooklyn Bridge Dimensions**

276 feet

119 feet

5,989 feet

*Diagram is not to scale

His bridge finally opened on May 23, 1883. The four biggest steel cables that hold up the roadway lessen the forces it feels. Each of those cables has about 3,600 miles (5,794 kilometers) of wire wrapped in it. Once the main cables were up, workers added about two thousand more steel wires to hold the roadway and walkway in place.

▲ The massive stone towers had to be erected first.

## Calculation Station

In building the Brooklyn Bridge, engineers often had to calculate **volume**. They did that, for instance, when building the two stone towers that form the backbone of the bridge. Volume is the amount of space filled by something with three dimensions.

To calculate the volume of a cube, use this formula: *volume = length x width x height*.

If the length, width, and height of a cube are all 11 inches, what is the volume of the cube? (Answer is on page 31.)

# Golden Gate Bridge

The Golden Gate Bridge in San Francisco has to stand against high winds and earthquakes. Bridge builder Joseph Strauss made the **center span**, the distance between the bridge towers, 4,200 feet (1,280 meters) long. The roadway sways just a bit in the wind. That way it does not collapse.

Work on the Golden Gate Bridge began in 1933. Workers used more than one million tons of concrete to build the bridge's two **anchorages**. Those are the huge blocks that hold the bridge's supporting cables. Construction was finished in 1937.

◀ Painters coated the 8,981-foot (2,737-kilometer) bridge in orange paint.

# Hands-On Math: Which Is Stronger?

Geometry helps make structures more stable. Complete this activity to find out which shape tends to be more stable, a triangle or a square.

## What You Will Need:
• 7 drinking straws          • 14 paper clips

## What to Do:

**1** To connect two straws, place the end of a paper clip into the end of straw.

**2** Hook a second paper clip to the first paper clip.

**3** Insert the end of the second paper clip into a second straw. Form a square and triangle.

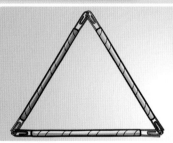

**4** Hold the shapes up, one by one. Press down on the top corners of each. Think about how much each shape twists and bends. How long before each one collapses?

## Explain Away
*Which shape was more stable? How might engineers use these shapes in building bridges? (Answer is on page 31.)*

# Water Wonders

People build dams to control the flow of water. A huge dam can change the face of Earth. Perhaps no dam changes its surroundings as much as the Three Gorges Dam in China. At 7,575 feet (2,309 meters) wide and more than 607 feet (185 meters) high, the dam is the largest ever.

## Three Gorges Dam

The dam crosses the mighty Yangtze River—the third longest river in the world. The dam holds back so much water that it creates a huge lake nearly 410 miles (660 kilometers) upstream. The lake holds an astounding 9.4 billion **cubic miles** (39.3 billion cubic kilometers) of water. Water passing through the dam will power much of China's electricity for years to come.

## Gravity Dam

Three Gorges Dam is a **gravity dam** built out of solid concrete. From above, a gravity dam's walls look straight. From the side, gravity dams are usually triangular in shape. As the weight of the water upstream pushes against the structure, the dam remains stable. Why? The dam's weight pushes down into the ground. That keeps the water from pushing the structure over.

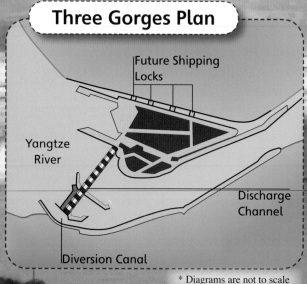

**Three Gorges Plan**

Future Shipping Locks

Yangtze River

Discharge Channel

Diversion Canal

\* Diagrams are not to scale

The Chinese needed 463,000 metric tons (about 2,025 pounds each) of steel to build the Three Gorges Dam. That's enough steel to build sixty-three Eiffel Towers.

▼ The dam changed how the water ran, so that people in 1,200 towns had to **relocate**.

## Calculation Station

Area is important when building dams. Area is the measure of a surface. In a square or a rectangle, area is equal to the width times the length. To make the calculation, make sure the length and height are in the same kinds of units before multiplying. When the width and length are both given in feet, the answer tells the square feet. What would be the square feet of a surface area 12 feet long by 24 inches wide? (Answer is on page 31.)

# Hoover Dam

Before the Hoover Dam changed the course of the Colorado River in 1936, the U.S. Southwest was very dry. It took a big dam to fix a big problem. Hoover Dam's main ingredient was concrete—4.5 million **cubic yards** (3.4 million cubic meters) of it.

To support the structure, engineers linked a series of columns shaped into **trapezoids**. A trapezoid is a four-sided figure with exactly two of its sides parallel. Each trapezoidal block was 5 feet (1.5 meters) thick.

If workers had built the dam by pouring the concrete at once, the temperature of the concrete would have been so hot that it would have taken 125 years to cool.

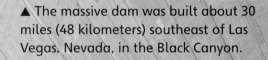
▲ The massive dam was built about 30 miles (48 kilometers) southeast of Las Vegas, Nevada, in the Black Canyon.

# Hands-On Math: Under Pressure

Try this activity to see water pressure in action.

## What You Will Need:

- Friend
- 2-liter plastic drink bottle
- Clay
- Scissors
- Drinking straw
- 12-inch ruler
- Marker
- Paper
- Water
- Pencil

## What to Do:

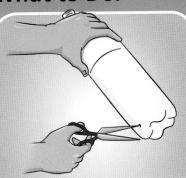

**1** Using scissors, have an adult cut a small hole in the bottle's bottom.

**2** Place a small bit of the straw in the hole. Seal the hole around the straw with clay.

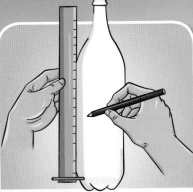

**3** Measure the bottle from the bottom up. Mark two, five, six, and eight inches.

**4** Place the bottle in a deep sink or bathtub. Place a finger over the hole of the straw at the bottom. Fill the bottle.

**5** Have your friend place the ruler under the straw, to "measure" water flowing down from the straw. Remove your finger from the straw.

**6** When the water level reaches eight inches in the bottle call out, "Eight!" Do that for each measurement mark.

### Explain Away

*What conclusion can you draw from the experiment? (Answer is on page 31.)*

# The Chunnel

If Napoleon (1769–1821) were alive, the French emperor would be amazed at the Chunnel. That is the tunnel that runs under the English Channel, linking France and Great Britain. When Napoleon was alive, Great Britain was France's enemy! Napoleon wanted to build such a tunnel, but people were afraid it would be used for one country to invade the other. It wasn't until after World War II that building the tunnel made sense to everyone.

Construction on the Chunnel began in 1987. Work was completed in 1994. The 31-mile (50 kilometer) tunnel makes traveling between London and Paris a breeze—just three hours long.

# A Boring Project

At its simplest, a tunnel is a hollow tube cut into the soil or stone. Engineers design tunnels to withstand forces like compression and **torsion**. Torsion is a force that twists material. The materials used must be strong enough to lessen these forces and others.

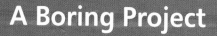

▲ *Chunnel* is an English nickname for the Channel Tunnel.

Workers used eleven boring machines to dig the tunnel through the soft rock. They had to dig out 8.7 million cubic yards (6.7 million cubic meters) of earth. The Chunnel is actually three tunnels in one. Two of the tubes are large enough for trains. The middle can be used as an escape route.

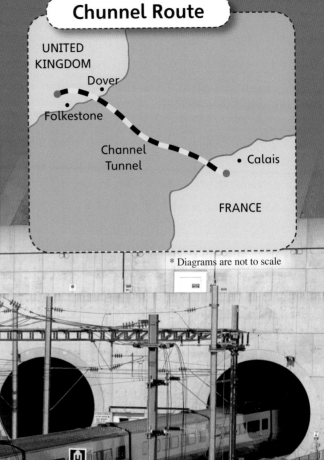

## Chunnel Route

UNITED KINGDOM

Dover

Folkestone

Channel Tunnel

Calais

FRANCE

* Diagrams are not to scale

## Calculation Station

In 2007, a Eurostar train traveled 192 miles per hour through the Chunnel. You can think of speed as the rate at which an object covers distance. The speed provided here is given in miles per hour. There are 60 minutes in an hour. So how many miles per minute would a train go at 192 miles per hour? (Answer is on page 31.)

# Chesapeake Bay Bridge-Tunnel

The Chesapeake Bay Bridge-Tunnel is in Virginia. It spans the open water where the Chesapeake Bay meets the Atlantic Ocean. It rises and dips over and under the water, with an assortment of tunnels, bridges, and humanmade islands.

The system is 17.6 miles (28 kilometers) long. It includes areas where ships can pass and two tunnels. The Thimble Shoal Tunnel is 15,738 feet (4,797 meters) long. The Chesapeake Channel Tunnel is 5,423 feet (1,653 meters) long. The tunnels are anchored to the islands. Huge rocks, each weighing up to 25 tons, protect the islands from the sea.

◀ More than 8,800 vehicles use the system each day. That number can reach 20,000 during the summer.

Engineers have to have good communication skills when they build things. Complete this activity to see how difficult building can be.

## What You Will Need:

- 10" high piece of cardboard with length at least 10"
- 2 books of the same size
- Paper
- Friend
- Ruler

## What to Do:

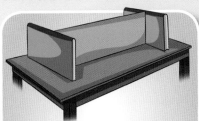

**1** Place the cardboard between two books, using pages to hold the cardboard edges. Be sure you and your partner cannot see what the other person is doing.

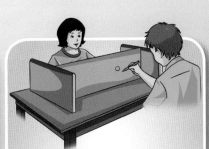

**2** Draw a circle about as large as a nickel on your side of the cardboard. Label that circle "Entrance A."

**3** Now your friend should do the same on the other side of the cardboard. Have your friend label that circle "Entrance B."

**4** Describe the location of Entrance A to your friend. Be exact. Your partner should then try drawing the other end of the tunnel on the other side of the board.

**5** Your friend should then describe the location of Entrance B. You should draw the other end of his or her tunnel on your side of the board.

**6** Carefully punch a small hole with a pen, showing where you think Entrance B is. Have your friend do the same for Entrance A.

## Explain Away

*How closely did the two ends of each tunnel match up? What conclusions can you draw from this activity about tunnel building? (Answer is on page 31.)*

# Glossary

**area** Measure of a surface of a three-dimensional figure.

**anchorage** Massive blocks that hold suspension bridges in place.

**borough** One of the five separate areas that form New York City.

**center span** Distance between the towers of a bridge.

**compression** Force that squeezes materials together.

**cubic mile** Volume of a cube with sides one mile long.

**cubic yard** Volume of cube with sides one yard long.

**cubit** Ancient measuring unit based on the size of a forearm.

**cylinder** Shape that is like a rounded tube.

**equation** A math term which means that the terms on the left add up to the same number as those to the right of the equal sign.

**equilateral** Equal length on all sides.

**geometry** A branch of math that deals with points, lines, angles, plane figures, and solid figures.

**gravity dam** A dam that resists the pull of Earth's gravity mainly through its own enormous weight.

**grid** Framework, often of crossed bars.

**relocate** To move to another place.

**right angle** Angle that measures exactly 90 degrees.

**stability** Firmness.

**stress** Measure of a force applied to a building.

**suspension bridge** Bridge that is hung from wires and towers, rather than or in addition to resting on posts.

**symmetry** Two sides that are in balance.

**tension** Stretched to stiffness.

**torsion** Force that twists material.

**three-dimensional** Having length, width, and height.

**two-dimensional** Having length and width.

**trapezoid** Four-sided figure with exactly two sides parallel.

**volume** Amount of space filled by a three-dimensional figure.

# Answer Key
## Calculation Station

p. 5: 36 divided by 12 = 3 inches per palm

p. 6: 252 × 252 = 63,504 sq. yards

p. 11: The right angle is the angle between side *a* and side *b*.

p. 15: 3,000 workers − 255 carpenters = 2,745 people

p. 19: 11 inches × 11 inches × 11 inches = 1,331 cubic inches

p. 23: 24 inches = 2 feet, so 12 feet × 2 feet = 24 square feet

p. 27: 192 miles divided by 60 minutes = 3.2 miles per minute

## Hands-On Math

p. 13: A paper column shored up with tape and sand is stronger than one without that support, so sand and tape increased the column's strength.

p. 17: The more toothpicks used to brace the tower, the stronger the tower; round towers are less stable than rectangular towers; for one thing, it is easier to brace four corners evenly than it is to brace a circle.

p. 21: The square shape is stronger than the triangle. The square can withstand greater pressure, so if engineers want to build a strong bridge or building, they would most likely use square shapes for braces instead of triangles.

p. 25: The greater the amount of water at the top of the bottle, the greater the flow of the water coming out of the bottom of the bottle because the weight of the water pushing down is greater when the bottle is filled.

p. 29: You can conclude that tunnel diggers have to give directions precisely if the tunnel entrances are to meet. Builders of all kinds need to communicate well.

# Index